NOVEMBER 8TH

Thanks for your
words of encouragement too...
I really appreciate it.

To Maggie
My dear friend
I speak Gal. 4:11 over
you...
God Bless You my
sister in the Lord.
I love you,

Val
Henderson
2·2012

NOVEMBER 8TH

VAL HENDERSON

Library of Congress Control Number: 2010904926
ISBN: Hardcover   978-1-4500-7716-3
                   Softcover   978-1-4500-7715-6
                   Ebook   978-1-4500-7717-0

This book was printed in the United States of America.

To order additional copies of this book, contact:
Xlibris Corporation
1-888-795-4274
www.Xlibris.com
Orders@Xlibris.com
79613

CONTENTS

I dedicate this book to my mother, Marie Turnbow and to all other women, children and men who have lost their lives because someone brutally murdered them. Also, to their families left behind to deal with the tragic loss of their loved one.

ACKNOWLEDGEMENTS

I want to thank my husband John, for the many hours he spent helping me create my book. He was a great strength to me while I worked through the challenges of writing this story.

To my brother Mike and all my friends, Carol, Claudia, Gale, Chance, Melissa, Carri, Jaye, David, Maggie, Allison, Shirley, Brenda and the many others who kept encouraging me to go forward with my book. I thank you all.

Many thanks to Deborah Collins for her wonderful suggestions that helped make my book complete and ready for publishing.

I thank all the people at Xlibris publishing that were involved in making my book publishing a good experience. You all did a great job.

To all the ladies that edited my book. I sincerely appreciate your help. You all did an excellent job!

INTRODUCTION

Val's powerful story of forgiveness has helped people of all ages and from all walks of life to rise to the challenge to take down roadblocks in their lives that has held them captive, keeping them from meeting their destiny.

Finding our destiny can sometimes be a bit confusing if we have not laid out a clear cut plan that will guide us down the path that has the answer. Sometimes, we must go back to the elementary things to resolve the issues that are stopping us from moving forward in a positive manner.

This story shines hope where there is none and teaches compassion, that gives freedom to forgive and move forward, leaving the roadblocks of the past behind. Making roadblocks a thing of the past.

CHAPTER 1

Nov. 8th

On the morning of November 8, 1967, at 9:30 A.M., the amplified sound of the Principal's voice broke the silence of the classrooms at my elementary school. The principal, Mr. Henderson, asked the teacher to release all four Turnbow children from class and have them come to his office. My teacher walked with me to the office and as we walked, she questioned me. She asked, "Why do you think you're going home?" A million thoughts were racing through my head. I told her, "I don't know." Though in my heart I feared something could be wrong with my mother. For some reason, my teacher asked again, "Why do you think you're going home?" I finally was able to get enough of my thoughts together to answer her. I told her mother had been in a small fender-bender recently and some of us kids were in the car when it happened. It had not been her fault, but the other driver. I told her we might be going home because she needs us to be witnesses that the accident was not her fault. Then my teacher got quite and didn't ask me any more questions. I sensed my teacher knew something had to be wrong. If all four Turnbow children were going home so early, when school had barely gotten underway that morning. Upon entering the office, Principal Henderson met us and simply told us that he and the school nurse were going to drive us home. There was no explanation why. I saw the nurse look at my teacher and give a look as to say, "Don't ask what is going on right now, you'll find out soon enough." My teacher nodded her head and remained quiet. She stood there with me and then stepped aside to watch us walk out of the office to go home. We only lived five minutes from school, but that morning, it seemed to take us forever to get home. All the way to our house, neither Mr.

Henderson nor the nurse said anything. The silence in the car was ominous; we knew something was terribly wrong at home. And we were right.

There are fourteen children in my family. I am number eleven. There were nine of us children still living at home in 1967. Eight months previously my parents, Joel and Marie Turnbow had gotten a divorce because my mother could no longer tolerate the physical abuse by my dad. After my parents divorce my dad started harassing my mother, threatening to kill her for divorcing him. As the principal's car turned the final corner toward home my heart sank. Dad's red pick up truck was parked in the driveway right behind mother's Rambler station wagon. There were police cars everywhere and the four of us burst into tears. The Principal drove us to the neighbor's house. As we stepped out of the car, news reporters, with their cameras, were taking pictures and people were standing out on their lawns, staring at us. My older sister, Nita, who stayed at home to baby sit the two youngest children, while my mother worked, came rushing out of the neighbor's house to hurry us inside, away from the crowd.

Nita sat us down on the couch and told us that our daddy had shot and murdered our mother and himself. After the news was broken to us about our parents, in our neighbor's house, I started crying again. Nita was standing on the front porch of our home and saw daddy shoot mother and himself. Years later, Nita told me that she could never get over what dad did. She said it was like someone was pushing a rewind button in her head and that scene kept playing over and over in her mind. It was my family's worst nightmare come to life. I remember just wanting to run away, escape, and make it all not real. I was eight years old and left an orphan, along with 8 other siblings.

Later that day, when all the news reporters and the crowd were gone, there was calm outside our house. My eleven year old brother Gary and I went to visit the place where my mother, had been killed in our neighbor's yard. There was a dried pool of blood on the ground. I got down on my knees and I took a tablespoon and a small brown paper bag and dug up the ground all around the dried blood. Then, I put the clod of dirt with the dried blood on it and stuck it in the bag. Gary said to me in a soft voice, "No, Valerie, don't save that dirt with momma's blood on it. Mother wouldn't want you to, she would want you to remember her alive and not dead." I was crying and I knew deep down in my little heart that Gary was right. So I reached down in the paper bag and pulled out the clod of dirt with my mother's blood on it and put it back into the hole which I had left in the ground. My heart was extremely sad I then stood up and my brother put his arm around me and we walked back towards our house together in silence with our heads hanging low. After that tragic day in our lives, none of my siblings or I ever spent the night at our house. It was just too emotionally painful to try and start our lives over in that house without our mother being there.

The older siblings that were married had decided to keep our family together. They were not going to put us younger ones in a children's home. When it came time to move everything out of our house, I remember standing outside in the driveway watching my older sisters and brothers loading furniture and other items on the back of a small, flat bed trailer. I could not even muster up the energy to go inside the house that day and help my family pack up our belongings. I kept having flash backs of mother in the house. It was too overwhelming for me to see them empty out our house and yet I did not want to live there any longer without my mother being there. I was distraught over all the new changes taking place in my life and was feeling unsure of my future. All I wanted was my mother.

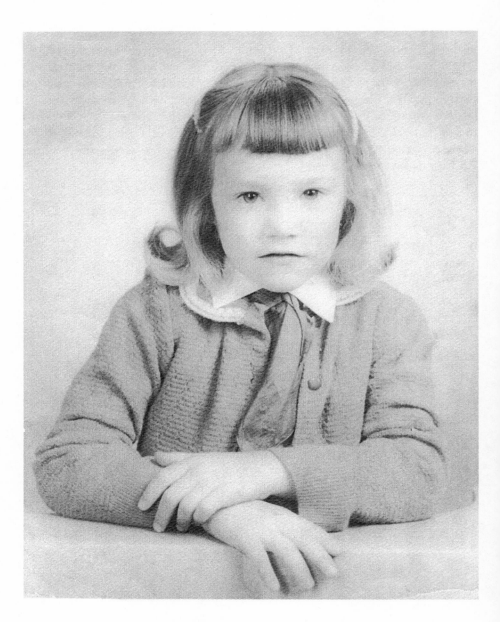

Val when she was 6 years old

CHAPTER 2

Every night

A younger sister and I shared a bed with our mother. Every night mother would go and get the gun out of the china cabinet, where she kept it locked during the day. Then she would stick it under her pillow and lay on her left side staring out the window. Mother never got enough rest. She was too busy worrying when the next time dad might try to harm her or her children. Mother would park the family car in front of the bedroom window so she could see or hear if dad came in the night to do something to it. It was clear my mother had to take extreme measures to protect us all from our abusive dad and now her ex-spouse. I remember one evening after my parents' deaths, we were at our house and there were people everywhere visiting our family. I had been staying at some friends home and so I had not been able to really mourn the loss of my mother. It was very difficult for me because I was like an infant still on a baby bottle and not ready for it to be taken away from me permanently. I finally found the time and courage to go alone to the bedroom I slept in at night with my mother and five sisters. I walked over to the bed I had shared with my mother and felt her side of the bed. Then I sat down on the foot of the bed and began crying uncontrollably, crying until I literally had no tears left. All I could do was make a mourning noise of pure brokenness. I knew I would never get to see my mother ever again, hear her sweet voice or sleep next to her either. My sister Nita came into the room upon hearing me weeping out of control. In spite of her own pain of losing mother, she took me in her arms and we cried together.

CHAPTER 3

My young mind

I can now understand how my young mind went into survival mode on the day of my parent's funerals. After their death, I did not see my dad until the day of his funeral. I remember at his funeral, there was hardly anyone there. I did not go to my dad's funeral to pay any respect. I went to his funeral to be sure he was dead. When it was time to walk past him in his casket I paused for a few minutes to get a good look. I looked real hard at his face and his chest. I wanted to be sure he was not breathing, that he was really dead. I looked for the gun wound to his head to be sure he had really killed himself. It was true. He was gone and I was glad. He was not going to come back and abuse our family any more. I was angry at him and the hate was flowing in my little heart. I did not cry at his funeral. I was filled with hatred and was glad he was gone. I was deeply saddened that he had taken my mother's life. He took the only parental stability I knew, out of my life; my mother who I loved more than life itself.

Later that day I went to my mother's funeral. I had gone to her viewing the night before at the funeral home and I remember walking up to her casket and looking at her lying there in that casket. She looked so peaceful. Her casket was in a very small viewing room and not more than 3 or 4 people could fit in the room. Outside the door you could sit and talk with your visitors. I waited until I could be alone with mother and then I went in the room to be with her. It was like she was just sleeping and I wanted to yell out to her. "Momma, wake up and come home with us. Wake up! Wake up!" Mother's body just laid there with no movement. I just kept hoping she would open her eyes and talk to me. Being eight years old, I didn't fully understand death until that moment in my life. I realized she wasn't going to get up and come home with us. She was gone forever! Forever! I was never going to see her again or have her hold me in her arms, kiss me goodnight and be able to talk to her again. It was painful to walk away from her casket and leave her at the funeral home. She looked so beautiful. She was wearing her pretty pink fuchsia dress with her blue teal scarf around her neck. I don't think I slept a wink that night because I couldn't stop thinking about mother.

At mother's funeral there was standing room only. We had her funeral services at our church. It was a big auditorium and when the pews were filled they let people come in stand along the walls. They ushered our family in last. When we walked into the auditorium I could not believe all the people lined up along the walls of the church. It was beautiful to see such a large gathering of people that had come to pay their respects to my mother and our family. It was such a blessing.

At the closing of her funeral, my family and I had to go first to walk by the casket. Because there was so many people at her funeral, we would have been all day letting everyone walk by her casket to pay their last respects. I really cannot remember how I even walked by her casket, I felt so much sorrow. I just wanted to fall on the ground and beat it out of pure sadness. My world was broken.

I was broken and so were all of my other siblings. One of my brothers stopped and fell on mother's chest, grabbing at her and pulling her up towards him. He was weeping uncontrollably and speaking to her, calling out, "Momma!, Momma!", over and over again. It was as though everything went into slow motion for me at that point. I lost all senses. I didn't know what to do. I was crying and someone took me by the hand and led me outside to a car. It was an Uncle. He had rescued me and took me away from the crowd and their staring faces. He sat in the back seat of the car with me. He put his arm around me and I leaned my head into the side of his chest and cried. I rode with my two uncles all the way to my mother's graveside. I could not even remove my head from the side of his chest or arms. I kept crying, on and off, all the way to the cemetery. I realize now that staying in my Uncle's arms was pure survival for me at that moment. I was scared of leaving my mother at the cemetery. After my mothers' service was finished, my two uncles took me to a convenient store and bought us something to drink. I remember going in with my uncle, who held me in his arms on the way to my mother's burial. My uncle put our cold drinks on the counter to pay for them and I noticed that one of the bottles was filled to the top of the cap. He caught me eyeing that cold drink and he asked me if I wanted that one to drink. I quickly said, "Yes!" He smiled and let me have that cold drink as mine. My Uncle saw me break a smile and I am sure that made him feel good, after all the crying I did on the way to the cemetery.

Many months after my parents' funerals, I would have literal visions at night in bed, of my dad chasing my mother around the cemetery, trying to kill her all over again. The vision always started with seeing two tomb stones with their names on them. Then that is when I would see my dad chasing my mother around the cemetery to try and kill her all over again. I was extremely afraid of the dark anyway and seeing that vision every night at bedtime was no sweet dream. I would yell to my sister to please let me sleep with the bedroom light on. I guess in my mind, I was afraid that my dad was going rise from the dead and come find my mother and kill her all over again. I was very protective of mother, even after her death. One day my sister asked me why was I so afraid of the dark and would not turn off the light. She pleaded with me to tell her. I finally got the nerve to tell her what I was seeing every time the light was off. She said, "Oh brother, that is the devil making you see those things and I am going to pray with you right now and you will never see that again." Well, it worked; I did not ever see those floating images in my bedroom at night again. Which could have been due partly to my sleeping with my head under the covers, to be sure I did not see those floating images ever again. I have spent years overcoming the death of my parents and the tragedy that came along with it. The cool thing is that I am doing it! Every day, even though it has been so many years ago, I am still putting my family's tragic past behind me and moving on with my life.

Lord, where ever there is void in my life. Please feel it with your unfailing love and compassion, so that I will not be alone in my despair.

CHAPTER 4

Staring Mode

A week or two later after my parent's funerals, my siblings and I were all back at work, and school, trying to get on with our lives. I, personally, would go into a staring mode. When I was in elementary school my teacher would call my sister and tell her I would just sit and stare into thin air, whether in the classroom or on the play ground. My sister told me years later, with tears flowing, that she did not know what to do get me stop the staring. When I was in fourth grade, we lived next door to some very sweet neighbors. They had two daughters and one was my age. I played with them almost every day. One evening, their parents came over and asked my sister if they could pay for me to go to gymnastics classes with their daughters. My sister said yes. Almost every day they would see me staring out the window for hours. So they felt it would help me if I had an activity to help occupy my time. You see, staring itself wasn't the problem; it was much deeper than that. I have discovered in my case, the staring was a way for me to suppress the sadness that was in me. I call it today, the sadder-than-sad mode. That was what had happened to me. My mind went into a survival mode of staring to prevent from having a total breakdown and going into a deep, severe depression. I didn't even know I was sitting and staring. I really believe my mind and spirit went into this staring mode to keep me going, even when I didn't feel like it.

It was a Saturday afternoon and their daughter and I were playing outside in the dirt. And for some reason or another, we got mad at each other. Which, children do when they are playing together sometimes and she yelled at me in anger, "The only reason my parents paid for you to go to gymnastics is because they felt sorry for you, because you're always staring out your bedroom window!

I stood up in a hurry and yelled back at her, "Na uh! That is not true!" Which, at that point, I ran inside to my bedroom and got in the closet and would not come out for several hours. I never told anybody about that day. My heart was broken and I was in deep despair of "sadder-than-sad." I eventually grew out of the staring mode. So, next time you see someone just sitting and staring for a while, go up and asked them if they want to talk about it. Tell them you have an ear to bend. It might just surprise you that they do need someone to talk to. Talking to someone you trust can sometimes helps work out the problem roadblocks in your life.

²⁴ You guide me with your counsel,
leading me to a glorious destiny.

Psalm 73:24 (New Living Translation)

CHAPTER 5

New Students

After a being back at school, a short time after my parents' funerals, one day on the playground, I met a little girl and her brother. They were new students and we quickly became friends. As we walked home together after school, the little girl started asking me how I felt about what my dad did to my mother. I had built up a lot of anger toward my father in the short time since his death. I assured the girl that I was going to hate my dad forever. I could never, ever forgive him for what he did. The little girl asked me if I would come home with her to meet her mother. Why not? I thought to myself. There is nobody waiting for me at home anymore. As we entered the living room the girl called for her mother to come and meet "the little girl from the newspaper." She continued yelling to her mother, "She says she's going to hate her dad forever." Well, the little girl's mother came rushing out of the bedroom and into the living room right away. She sat me down on the couch and put her arm around me and said, "Oh no, honey, you need to forgive your dad for what he did." It would take me years to realize the wisdom of her words.

[14] I will praise You, for I am fearfully *and* wonderfully made;[a]
Marvelous are Your works,
And *that* my soul knows very well.
[15] My frame was not hidden from You,
When I was made in secret,
And skillfully wrought in the lowest parts of the earth.
[16] Your eyes saw my substance, being yet unformed.
And in Your book they all were written,
The days fashioned for me,
When *as yet there were* none of them.

[17] How precious also are Your thoughts to me, O God!
How great is the sum of them!
[18] *If* I should count them, they would be more in number than the sand;
When I awake, I am still with You.

Psalm 139:14-18 (New King James Version)

CHAPTER 6

1982

In 1982, almost fifteen years later, while leafing through a local faith based yellow pages, I came across an article called, "The Six Steps to Salvation," a simple outline of how to receive the Lord into your heart. I skimmed through the article and quickly concluded that it did not apply to me. Besides, I was a person of good moral values, had been reared by a loving, caring Christian mother, and we regularly went to church, so I really did not think I needed Him in my heart. Then about two weeks later, I had a terrible nightmare in which I was shoveling coal in hell's furnace, while a red devil watched over me. When I woke up from this dream, I knew exactly what I had to do. I got up out of bed, grabbed the yellow pages, went into the bathroom, and knelt down on the rug on the floor. I read through, "The Six Steps of Salvation" again, and when I came to the last step, it said "Now just admit to God you are a sinner." It was at that point I realized I was a sinner. Even though I had been a "good" person all my life, I still needed the Lord in my heart. Even though my sins were small; gossiping, telling an occasional white lie, without the Lord in my heart, I was as far away from the Heavenly Father as the most brutal murderer. Suddenly, my dream about shoveling in hell made sense: In my own way I was unknowingly serving Satan, not the Father. I asked the Father for forgiveness of all my sins that morning, and His mercy poured out on me. He met me right where I was, and I accepted the Lord into my heart. I was His. There was no turning back.

What happened to me next was extraordinary! It was bedtime and my husband turned on the Master bathroom light for me, because I always slept with the light on. I said to him, "Turn the light off, the Lord had taken my fear of the dark away." My husband was amazed! There is one thing I can say for my husband, he never ridiculed me for being afraid of the dark. He'd always say to me, "One day you will not be afraid of the dark and you will sleep with the light off." He was right! The Heavenly Father had healed me of my fear of the dark. I grew up being extremely afraid of the dark because of my dad. My dad would usually wait until dark to start his abuse. I would lay awake in bed with tears in my eyes at night, listening to my dad hitting my mother and I could hear her yelling at him to stop. Then later, my dad would leave the house for awhile and my mother would come rushing in the bedrooms to hurry us children out of bed, to flee in the night, from dad. We would have to hide down alleys and in bushes until we could get someone to come and pick us up and take us to a safe place to hide. My life at home, in those days, was a constant roller coaster. I was emotionally overwhelmed and the stress of the abuse by my dad caused me many years of shame and sadness, until I finally learned to start getting rid of the baggage my dad had caused in my life.

CHAPTER 7

1983

A year later, in 1983, I was watching a faith based talk show on television, and there was this woman telling the story of her tragic, family camping trip. She and her husband had slept in one tent and her children, two teens and a five-year-old daughter, had slept in another. During the night someone cut a slit in the children's tent and pulled the youngest daughter out, kidnapping her. The woman said that when she woke up and discovered what had happened, she cried out to the Father to please help her and her family find their daughter. The police explained to her that the chances of the girl being alive weren't good, but she told the Father that she needed to know where her daughter was—even if she was dead. She also asked the Father to tell her who it was that took her daughter. Finally, after much prayer, the Father answered her prayers about finding their daughter, although it brought even more tragic news when the authorities did find her.

Unfortunately, the news would be that their daughter had been raped and murdered by her perpetrator. Later, the man who had violated the little girl was caught and sentenced to prison for the crime he committed. After the funeral and the trial, and the murderer safely behind bars, the woman and her family thought they would finally be able to get on with their lives. However, before long the woman and her husband had the strong sense that God wanted them to forgive the man for what he did to their little girl. So they visited the man in prison and told him that they forgave him for what he did to their daughter. They ended up befriending the man and started having bible studies with him. Before long, the man accepted the Lord into his heart and his life started changing, all because that woman and her husband were obedient to the Father and chose to forgive, instead of letting unforgiveness, bitterness, and hate rule their lives. The woman's forgiveness story struck a chord in my heart and I knew what I had to do. I turned off the television and went to my bedroom and knelt down on the floor on the side of the bed. I broke down and started crying out loud to the Father. I said, "Father please forgive me for not forgiving my dad for murdering mother and himself and all the other things he did to hurt our family." I asked Him to let my dad know that I forgave him." Then a voice within me said, "No, you tell him yourself, just as if he was here listening." So I did.

I said out loud, "Daddy, I forgive you for killing mother and yourself and all the other mean things you did to hurt our family, too." I continued on, "And, Daddy . . . I love you." I couldn't believe the words were coming out of my mouth, because in all the eight years I had spent with dad, he never once told me he loved me, nor I him. He never even gave me a hug. It's sad to me that I had to learn to love my dad after he was dead and gone. But once I had forgiven him, by the Father's grace I was able to really start growing in my faith and moving on with my life. Like the woman who forgave her daughter's murderer and rapist, I had experienced the same incredible power of forgiveness. My dad was wrong for what he did, and there is no excuse for his action. I can never turn back the pages of time, but in spite of my family's tragedy, I am able to look forward and make the most of my life, regardless of the shame that my dad's actions brought my family.

CHAPTER 8

Suicide

In January 1979 and in December 1989, almost ten years apart, two of my older brothers committed suicide. Neither of my brothers fully recovered from our parents brutal deaths. They both felt they had let our mother down, because they could not be at home on that day to protect her. They carried a very deep shame and guilt in their hearts for what dad did to mother. I had talked, to my brother Gary, about how he felt just three months before he took his life in December, 1989. I found out that daddy tried to use Gary to carry out his evil deed against mother. On the day before our parents' deaths, dad had picked Gary up from the house, while mother was at work. Dad did not get mom's permission to take Gary with him. Later that evening, when dad returned Gary to the house, he told him to lock the dogs up in to the garage, unlock the back door and leave off the back porch light, before we all went to bed that evening. Well, Gary being only 11 years old, not catching on to what dad was up to, did as he was told. Dad was always coaching Gary to misbehave and be rebellious to mother. Fortunately, we had an older teenage brother, who was working at the local theater a few blocks away from home. He got off work around 11pm and when he arrived at home, he found the dogs put up, the back porch light off and the back door unlocked. He thought mom must have forgotten to make sure the house was secure before going to bed. So he let out the dogs in the backyard, turned on the porch light and locked the back door. There is no telling what my dad was going to do that night. It frightens me to think my dad could have been planning to kill us all.

However, God was watching over us and he protected us children from my dad's evil plans. So now, you can better understand why my brother Gary was blaming himself for mom's death. Because he deliberately did not tell her what dad told him to do that night before their deaths. I tried hard to get my brother to forgive himself for obeying dad and reminded him that he was only eleven years old! Shame on our dad for using him to carry out his evil plans. I was saying everything I could think of to convince Gary it was not his fault that daddy had killed mother.

I remember that day as if it was yesterday. We were standing in my living room talking and I was pleading with my brother not to blame himself for dad's actions. He fell in my arms weeping uncontrollably and let me know that the burden was too heavy for him to bear. I held Gary in my arms, with his head on my shoulders and we both cried together, sharing the pain he was going through emotionally. I prayed with him and let him know that I loved him dearly. Sometimes, life is too hard to explain. I can only point people in such emotional stress to the Father. He is our true answer. Seeking His wisdom is what we must do to fight the battle that is within us.

My Brother Gary and I, one year before his death in 1989.

CHAPTER 9

Happy Moments

I miss my brothers and my mother so much. I miss all their smiling faces and the closeness I had with each of them, in my own special way. I want you to know that there were some happy moments in our lives, even though they might have been far and few between. I'll begin the first happy story with, Gary and I, and how we used to hang out together a lot in our teenage years. He had quit school, got his GED and went into the Marines.

The summer before he went into the service, I was living in Austin, Texas, with an older sister and her husband. I went to Dallas to visit with another older sister and her husband for two weeks. Gary and I hung out together so much while I was in town, that people thought we were boyfriend and girlfriend. To keep people from thinking that, we went and had the words, "She's my sister" printed on a t-shirt for Gary and on my t-shirt we had printed, "He's my brother." It was great! We had our sister take a picture of us in our t-shirts. Everyone that saw our shirts loved them. I have so many happy memories of my brother Gary. I don't think Gary really ever understood how dear he was to my heart. We got along well and it was sad, when I got married, we grew apart in our closeness to one another. I miss my brother's friendship and joking behavior. He was a good brother to me.

An older brother than Gary and I, committed suicide in 1979, holds a special place in my heart as well. One of my most fond memories of him was when he bought a soup-up, 1968 Chevy Camero. It is one of my favorite cars on the face of the earth! His car was blue with wide pin-stripes on the hood and across the trunk of the car. The back end of the car was slightly jacked up and he had mag-wheels on all four tires. It was a stick shift and I am not sure what type of

Picture of Gary and I with Tee-shirts on.

engine it had under the hood. Whatever it was, it was fast and that is the only way he would drive his car. I would ride with him a lot in that car, in fact, he'd let me go with him racing down the freeway, whenever he would race another of our brothers, in his hot rod, Chevy.

I would get so scared of how fast my brother was driving, that I would get down in the back seat floorboard, right behind the drivers seat and put my fingers in my ears and wait for it all to be over with. Then, when the race was over I would come up out of the floorboard and ask my brother who won. We would laugh and laugh about who won. I am not sure anyone really ever won those races. It was really not for winning, as much as it was just to show off how fast each others cars could go. It is amazing that neither one of them ever got pulled over by a police while they were racing. I miss those days of hanging out with my brother. He was dear to my heart and was a good brother to me.

The happy memories with my Mother are far too many to write about in this book. However, I will share with you a fun, family moment I remember with her in 1966. Whenever I had to stay home from school, due sickness or for some other reason, my mother would wait until all the older siblings were gone to school in the morning time. Then, after she had all her morning chores done, she would take us younger children into the den and turn on the radio. Mother would wait until her two favorite songs, "Sweet Pea" by Tommy Roe and the "Yellow Submarine", by the Beatles, to come on and then we'd all start dancing to the songs. Mother would laugh and dance with us children and we would sing to the words of the songs and be dancing all around her. She would sometimes hold our hand and twirl us around. We had a blast with her! It was always good to see my mother happy. And whenever I think of her, I think of those happy moments of singing and dancing on those old, wood floors in the den. Our house was the favorite house on the block because my mother didn't mind children being around. What were a few more neighbor kids visiting when she already had fourteen of her own? Mother was super kind, thoughtful, and generous. She never met a stranger. Everyone that met mother usually fell in love with her sweet temperament. I never heard her talk bad about anyone, including our dad. If she caught one of her children talking bad about our dad, she would immediately tell them to quit. Mother would say, "That is your father and no matter what he has done to me, you do not talk about him in that way." My mother, Marie Turnbow was Super mom! I love her and miss her greatly. I know she is in heaven with the Father, no doubt.

Val's parents in happier times

Val's parents 1955

Valerie

Hi Maggie,

Hope you are
feeling better...
Keeping you
in my prayers
Love you,
Val

CHAPTER 10

Long after

Long after I had forgiven my dad for taking his and mother's life I still had so many questions of why would he do such an awful thing to our family? One night, I called my dad's younger brother and asked him many questions about my dad. I told him I was still trying to understand my dad and I needed to know if my parents were ever happily married. My uncle told me that my parents met at a fair and it was love at first sight for the both of them, you could not ever find them apart from one another. Dad treated mother with great kindness and sincere love. He said that dad had gotten drafted in the service in WWII and was on a ship, crossing the ocean to go fight in the war. However, the war ended while he was on the ship. The service sent my dad to Okinawa, Japan, for two years and he became a military policeman while there. By surprise, one of his brothers had been sent there also and dad got to be stationed there with him. When dad returned home from the service overseas he had changed, like night and day. When he had left to go fight in the war, he was kind and had a gentle soul and never treated my mother mean or ever hit her. Then, upon returning home after two years of being in the service, he had become mean and bitter. He had become physically and verbally abusive to mother.

It is sad that my dad did not know how to conform back to civilian life after the military. He forgot how to treat those he loved most. My dad had become dead on the inside. I can now understand, to some extent, how he became non-caring to the civilian life. The service needed him to be mean and tough for protection reasons against our enemies. His family still needed him to be the gentle man that he was before he went into the service. Somehow my dad was having a hard time adjusting back to plain old civilian life.

One example of this is he would sometimes blame mother for things that really were not worth fighting about, or even discussing. On a summer day, which was a Saturday when I was five years old, my brother Gary and I were called into lunch by our mother. Dad and mother sat at opposite ends of the table and Gary and I sat across the table from each other. I do not know where all my other brothers and sisters were. All I remember is that Gary sat down at the table in front of his plate of food. In a very short time, Gary having his elbows upon the table, Dad immediately blamed mother for him having his elbows on the table. Dad made Gary get up and go stand in the kitchen where he took his belt and started hitting Gary, extremely hard with the belt. In fact, it was so hard that mother intervened and told dad to stop hitting him. Mother even grabbed at the belt in flight. Dad then proceeded to turn the belt on mother and started beating her with it. I ran from the table towards the kitchen screaming for my dad to stop hitting momma and Gary.

I was trying my best to grab the belt out of my dad's hands and screaming at him to stop all at the same time. My dad finally stopped hitting them and then told my mother that Gary and I were to go sit outside, in our little metal chairs, in the middle of the backyard until he gave the permission for us get up. Dad even left to go somewhere and warned mother that we better not get up from those chairs while he was gone or she would be the one to pay for it. Gary and I sat out there in that backyard, with no shade, in the heat of summer until the sun set. As you know, the sun does not set until 9:00 P.M. during the summer. Mother stood at the kitchen window watching us in pure mental anguish. The look on her face that day broke my heart. I knew mother felt hopeless. She did allow us to get up to get water and go to the bathroom, whenever we needed to. Gary tried hard to get me to go inside out of the heat, but I would not. I would have rather taken a thousand beatings for my mother and Gary that day, than to see either of them to be beaten by my dad ever again. I think dad thought military style of punishment was good for all people, except for him, of course. Some of my siblings would tell you that our daddy was mean most of the time. Sometimes, I put my elbows on the kitchen table when I am eating, in loving memory of my brother Gary.

I believe somewhere inside my dad, there was a gentler side of him from his past and I wanted it to be there for me, his daughter. I wanted to be daddy's little girl and I am sure there was a time I was.

"Sometimes, I put my elbows on the kitchen table when I am eating, in loving memory of my brother Gary."

Dad could be gentle when he needed to be, it just was not often enough. I remember a very special moment I had with my dad when I was about 3 or 4 years old. He worked for the railroad and had to be to work at 6 A.M. He would take me out to the backyard with him while he sat on the back porch and drank his morning coffee, before he went to work. Dad would turn on the back porch light, because it would still be dark and he would take my little doll stroller outside and sit it down in the yard. I would take my baby doll and put it in the stroller. Which I would then push around the backyard, while my daddy watched me and looked at the morning paper, while drinking his coffee. It was always a very special moment that I looked forward to with him. I would stand up in the seat next to daddy, while he drove, when we took him to work. I even remember many times going to sleep on his shoulders and listening to his voice through his chest. There was always comfort in falling asleep listening to my daddy's voice. It must have made me feel safe and loved in those days, as I felt I was daddy's little girl. I miss having a dad in my life. I miss having a grandfather for my children. I am grateful for the short time I did have with my dad and to know that there was some gentler moments in his life, that I was able to enjoy with him.

Thinking back to my brother Gary, I now know that all he ever wanted was to be daddy's little boy and make him proud. Gary would have done anything that dad asked of him. Now it is easier for me to understand why Gary was overwhelmed with grief and a troubled spirit within himself; he thought he could earn his daddy's love by his actions. When Gary came to realization that his dad, whom he looked up to, had used him to plot murder against his own mother, it brought his world of love for dad and that feeling of being daddy's little boy to a crashing halt. Gary was horrified he had played right into daddy's sweet talk, which was nothing but deception. I feel terribly sad for my brother. I feel very strongly that both of my brothers, are in heaven. I know that the Heavenly Father can still have compassion, even unto death.

I do not believe my dad felt loved by his family. He knew he had already caused so much damage by his behavior, that when he did apologize, it had become empty words to all of our ears. We knew he would only change for a short time and then be back to his abusive ways again. No doubt that my dad probably needed to be retrained in how to treat civilians, after the Military service life. My dad had only a fourth grade education. I am sure he felt somewhat cheated in his own life and he hadn't realized it until he was in the armed services. I am not trying to make any excuses for what my dad did. He is what he was, a murderer. That can never be changed and that is why even today, although I can say I do love my dad, I am still trying to define my love for him. Although I did not have a dad in my life that could influence me in a positive manner, the Heavenly Father sent a couple of men in my life that were good role models in their own special way. I will share that with you in the next chapter.

"I know that the Heavenly Father can still have compassion, even unto death."

CHAPTER 11

Brother-in-laws

I had two brothers-in-laws who showed love and compassion in my life when I was growing up. The first is my sister's husband, the sister that raised me, who was always there for our family whenever my mother needed him to be. Then after my parent's deaths, I went to live with them. He was funny and very goal oriented when it came to making money. He was a top shoe salesman where he worked and then later in life, he went on to work for other companies, where he excelled even greater in sales. Living around him was a very good thing for me. He kept me reaching higher and higher in my own life. He encouraged spiritual growth, prayed at the dinner table with us and helped my sister take good care of me and a younger sister who lived with them also. He showed me that I could do anything I wanted in life so long as I put forth a strong effort to make it happen. In high school, I ended up winning some sales awards in a class I was in. I was always trying my best. I am sure to some of my friends, it seemed I had everything going well for me. On the inside of me, however, things weren't going so well. I was smiling on the outside but falling down on the inside. You already know my past and how I overcame it. I believe I have been successful because of the Heavenly Father sending people like my brothers-in-law into my life to encourage me in a positive manner. They gave me resources that pointed me in the right direction, even though I may have struggled along the way, to see the light at the end of the tunnel.

The second brother-in-law that the Father used to encourage me was another older sister's husband. I use to spend a lot of time with him and my sister on the weekends. I would spend the night with them and during the summer, I would spend a week with them. My sister's husband use to take me fishing with him and my sister often. Though my sister didn't fish, she would come along for just the enjoyment of being with her husband. It meant a lot to me for him to take me fishing with them. (*When ever my dad would go fishing, he would take my brothers and my mother. I always had to stay home. I have often thought that if my dad would have known what a good fisherman I was, he would have let me come along on his fishing trips.*) We three had many fun filled days of just going out fishing and having a picnic.

One time, we all went fishing with his brother and his uncle. My sister stayed on the shore with the other women and all the guys took me with them in the fishing boat. It was hilarious! The guys gave me, the 10 year old, a cane pole to fish with and they all had their fancy fishing reels. I was sitting in the back of the boat with my cane pole fishing and the craziest thing happened; I started catching fish. I caught up to eight fish that day and the guys did not ever catch one fish. Later in life, as recent as 2009, I was at a nieces birthday party and his brother was there. I went up to him and asked if he remembered me and that day we all went fishing, and he the other guys did not catch anything. He laughed and said, "Yes, I do remember and is why I quit fishing. Now the only fish he catches is at the grocery store. I like fish that are already caught, cleaned and ready to be cooked to eat." It was fun talking about those fishing days. I am grateful that my brother-in-law, taught me to fish. That gave me confidence to try other new hobbies.

So you really don't know how you will touch someone else's life by just the simple things you talk with them about and do with them. My brothers-in-laws never knew the importance of the simple guidance that they were giving me while I grew up fatherless. Having them around was what my life needed. It kept me balanced in my unsure world.

Chapter 12

Survival

Living in an unsure world was not my cup of tea as a child. As I've grown and matured in my thinking, I can look back and see how I've learned survival from my mother, because of being given an unsure world at the age of eight. My mother did whatever it took to overcome her abusive husband. After years of taking his abuse, she finally realized he wasn't going to change and it was time for her to come up with a plan that would help her and her children out of his abusive control. First, mother bought a gun for herself and obtained a restraining order to help protect her against dad. One day that gun did help stop dad from trying to force his way into our house. Dad had stop by the house and he insisted that he was just dropping off some bags of fruit for his family. I could see that worried look in mothers face. Once again, she told dad to leave through the front screen door and reminded him she had a restraining order against him and he was not even suppose to be near her. Dad just turned around to go back to his truck to get the fruit. I remember that he had set some oranges on the ground and walked to the back of his truck, to possibly get more fruit out of it. While he went to the back of his truck mother went and got her gun out of the china cabinet where she kept it safe and locked up during the day. She came back to door and yelled for dad to leave and he would not. So mother fired the gun towards the ground near my dad. Dad ran behind the truck and yelled, "Marie, I cannot believe you just tried to shot me." She said, "Virgil, I told you to leave, now leave!" He jumped into his truck and took off. I remember some of my siblings walked out to the bag of oranges and picked them up and started throwing them out in the street. I know mother would have never fired that gun at my dad if she had not felt desperate. She was not a violent person and was always kind to people. I know that day did not bring any joy to my mother. She was a petite woman and could not protect herself from dad's abuse. So that day, she was able to finally defend her self before any physical abuse begun. It was a small victory for her. One of my older sisters, who was a teenager at the time, can not remember mom firing her gun at dad. I reminded her that how else would dad have left in such a hurry. Believe me, our mother could not convinced him to leave any other way. Words did not mean anything to my dad. Mother always used money as an excuse to stay married to dad. It was understandable with so many children to feed, clothe and take care of financially. Mother came up with a plan to put us in a local children's home so that she could take better care of us.

Mother approached the children's home and requested they take us in, but what happened next, was awesome! The director of the home told my mother that they would pay her a monthly support check to help take care of her children so that she could keep them at home with her. What a break! It was just what mother needed because dad was not paying child support. Dad was trying to break mother's spirit so she would have to come back to him. Mother worked for a company sewing clothes and knew that her paycheck alone would not bring in enough income to support us. So she went to work for a realtor in the evenings and started studying to get her realtor license.

Believe me, that did not go over big with my dad. It made him blistering mad. Because it meant that mother had come up with a plan to overcome her financial dependence on him and her plan was working. That is when dad knew, once the divorce was final, there was no turning back for mother. She was making it out of the abuse and without losing her children to him. Praise the Heavenly Father that my mother went into survival mode.

CHAPTER 13

Tears of Joy

I have cried many tears of joy over the past years. I am a survivor of suicide. There have been four suicides in my family. Sometimes, I count my mother's death as a suicide because of her unselfish act of finding the courage to leave her abusive husband, so that she or her children did not have to suffer at the hand of his abuse anymore. She knew dad would never leave her alone, even after their divorce was final. I am glad she was not afraid anymore to take a chance and set us all free from his bondage. Mother's unselfish act has certainly paid off in all her children's lives today. Each of us has something unique to give back to others through our family's tragic past.

In 2000, a nephew was the fourth suicide in our family. He was going through some issues in his life and they had overwhelmed him. One evening he decided to take his own life, by hanging himself in his bedroom closet. I was living in Minnesota at the time and I received the call at 10:00 p.m. at night. My sister called to tell me the news about our nephew and that he was in ICU. The doctors were coming out to call everyone into the family room. I told my sister, "I need to hang up the phone right now. I need to pray." We said our good-bye and I hung up the phone. I was down in my basement and my son was upstairs with his friend visiting. I immediately forgot who was home or listening and went to praying fervently for my nephew. I yelled out to God, "No more!," I said again, "no more suicides in our family, God.! No more!" I prayed that the Heavenly Father would not let him die. I yelled out to my nephew, calling out his name. Telling him to rise up off that hospital bed and live! He had not met his destiny yet! He was too young to die. I did not know that my family in Texas was praying the very same kind of prayer at the hospital.

Although, we were all 1000 miles apart, our fervent prayers were going up to the Lord, in one accord.

I called the youth pastor at our church and asked him and his wife to please come and pray with me about my nephew. They both came over around 5:00 a.m. and we stayed in the basement office and prayed. The youth pastor opened his bible and turned to Psalms and started singing scriptures to my nephew and put his name in the verses, lifting his voice up to the Lord for my nephew. It was beautiful! We all cried and prayed. While we were praying I had a vision and saw the Lord standing beside my nephew's hospital bed, speaking to him and telling him to rise up. I knew when I saw that vision I could stop praying for my nephew. I told the youth pastor and his wife we could stop praying now, my nephew was going to be alright. The Lord was standing beside his bed and talking to him and everything was going to be alright, I felt peace come over me and the whole situation.

I called my best friend in Texas, to tell her about my nephew because she has known my family since the early 1980's. She asked me if she could go up to the hospital and sing Psalms over my nephew. I told her I was sure his parents would appreciate her thoughtful gesture and so she went. It was amazing because she did not know that the youth pastor had just done the same thing from our office in Minnesota. So as you can see, it was clearly the Lord speaking to all our hearts from Texas to Minnesota, to help get my nephew well and out of that hospital in less than 24 hours. My husband, John and I drove 15 hours the next day to eat lunch with him. Later on, I found out that my nephew had seen the Lord standing beside his hospital bed. The Lord told him, "You asked the Heavenly Father to let you kill yourself, you had asked Him to let me take your life and not even I can take your life without the Heavenly Father's permission."

Wow! Not even our Messiah can take our life without the Father's permission. How powerful that is . . . really think about it. There is hope in this life; it is an unseen hope that we each have if we only ask the Heavenly Father. His wisdom is beyond human understanding. Today, I am telling you, that I honestly cry tears of joy over my family's tragic past. Hope is the substance not seen and the future of our joy can be in even a hopeless situation. God is bigger than any roadblock or obstacle that stands in the way of our hope. Living life by faith is truly what I have learned to do. So many times, just when I feel like I will not make it, I pray and God shows up on the scene. Then I say, "No more, God! No more of me, only you. Take the steering wheel, your wisdom is greater than mine." Scriptures states, "Lean not into your own understanding, but His"

Recently, one of my sisters told me that she believed God raised our nephew from his death bed, because her and some other family members prayed together after our brother Gary committed suicide in 1989. The words they prayed were, "No More suicides in our family, God!" I personally think that is awesome! In the fall of 2009, God told me that was actually why our nephew wasn't able to die from committing suicide, because our family said, **"No more!"** God showed up when we all finally had enough of ourselves, trying to control the situation. It doesn't matter when those words were prayed. What matters is that they were prayed.

CHAPTER 14

Roadblocks

I was a flight attendant in 1999. It was my dream job. However, I was not able to work because of a work related injury. God gave me hope through giving me the "Roadblock Message". It was an added bonus to my forgiveness story. I was living in Minnesota at the time and one afternoon, I was sitting on the couch in my basement. I cried out to God and said to Him, "I was totally useless to Him, I was not able to do much physically." He plainly told me, "Just be quite, I do not want to hear it. Valerie, if you want me to use you in the ministry, I will, regardless of your disability. Are you willing?" I told him, "Yes! What do you want me to do?" He said, "Draw a roadblock with orange and white strips and put ember lights on it." And so I did. Then He said to me, "Valerie, each orange stripe represents sin that keeps people from having a relationship with Me or an issue that is stopping them from moving forward in a positive manner with their life." He continued on, "Tell people I want them to take down their roadblocks and take up their cross and follow me daily. In the next following chapters I will continue to explain the complete message of the Roadblock. It is uniquely designed to have no barriers when it comes to gender or age.

The Roadblock program is a simple plan to help you resolve your negative issues. (*It takes you back to the elementary of things, resolving issues in your everyday routine.*) *Keep* reading the Word and seeking the Father's wisdom with knowledge and understanding, for every area of your life. Keep reading the Word, because within its pages is a wealth of wisdom from the Father. So whenever in doubt,

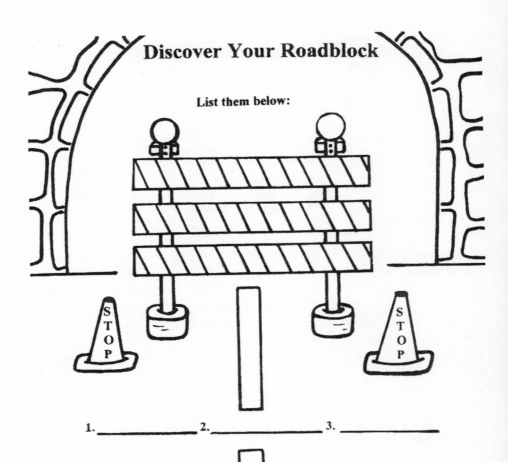

Discover Your Roadblock

List them below:

1._____ 2._____ 3._____

What is stopping you from moving forward?

for any area of your life, read the Word. It will help you find your way to the Keeper of the gate, He bears all wisdom. I hope that after reading this book you will find solid, good, positive solutions to taking down your roadblocks and moving forward in positive manner. Once you begin the process of changing, keep the wheels in motion. The road for you to overcome may not be easy. You may have valleys and hills to climb to get there, but you will survive. Just keep telling yourself you will make it, because now you are facing truth in your life and you're willing to take down the pride in your life and make it happen. There was a saying we used when I was in medical assisting school; "Whatever it takes!" Believe me that was the perfect thing for our class to use as our motto. At exam time, we needed to be reminded of that motto. It is a good saying to use in our everyday lives.

You will find it is true that, practice makes perfect. It will get easier as you bring down every negative that is keeping you from going forward in a positive manner. The more you practice taking down roadblocks, the more it will become a lifestyle that is incorporated into your everyday routine.

My mother knew that the road was going to be tough but survival mode was one of the many keys to staying focused on making her new positive changes come true. Survival attitude would have to become incorporated into her everyday routine, in order for it to become a life style for her and it can be one for you, too. Keep moving forward, you will find a way through your issues. There is light at the end of the tunnel. Remember the saying, that it takes a negative and positive charge to make a battery work. Go into survival mode and win the battle within yourself. Go. Let go and the Father will do the rest.

Not all roadblocks are bad in our lives. They can represent protection as well as changes that need to take place before we can move forward in a particular direction. Roadblocks can protect us from the hidden dangers ahead in our lives. Think of times in your life that it seemed no matter how hard you tried to go forward with certain things and yet it seemed there were roadblocks in every direction stopping you.

God has a way of preventing us from moving forward at times, until we fix the troubled areas in our lives that can cause us to go off the road. The path we have been following may be in need of repair before we can continue forward. This is why I encourage you to write down the roadblocks that are keeping you bound. Then write down a positive action that will counteract those negative roadblocks. Put your positive plan into action and see what happens next.

In His mercy, we will find His forgiveness.

CHAPTER 15

Right Now

Right now you may be asking yourself, how can you begin your journey toward dropping the issues in your own life, that have been keeping you from moving forward in a positive manner and accepting the Lord in your heart? Surprisingly, it's all pretty simple. First, you must realize that you are nothing without God, our heavenly Father; an empty shell, and you need Him in your heart and life. No matter whom you are, rich or poor, skinny or fat, a good person or a bad person, male or female, young or old, black or white, a movie star or just Jane or John Doe, Romans 3:23 says, "We all have fallen short of the glory (honor) of God."

Like me, you may need to forgive someone for the wrong he or she has done to you, before you can fully accept the Father's forgiveness. Or maybe, you just need to forgive yourself for the wrong things you have done to yourself and others. We serve a big and mighty God and there are no issues or sin that you or I have committed that is bigger than Him and His forgiveness. Matthew 6:14-15, is just one of the many passages of scriptures that show how important it is to forgive: "For if you forgive men their trespasses, you're heavenly Father will also forgive you. But if you do not forgive men their trespasses, neither will your Father forgive your trespasses." So as you can see, it is very important to forgive those who have wronged you. Ephesians 4:30-32 says, "And grieve not the Holy (set a-part) Spirit of God, whereby you are sealed until the day of redemption. Let all bitterness, and wrath, and anger, and clamor, and evil speaking, be put away from you, all malice: and be kind one to another, tenderhearted, forgiving one another, even as He has forgiven you . . ."

CHAPTER 16

Relationship

A relationship with your heavenly Father is much easier than you may think. Let's take down that roadblock of sin and any issues standing in your way and help you take up your cross and follow Him, by first writing down on the "Go" worksheet, on the following page, how you are going to counteract the negative with a positive action. Luke 9:23 says, "If anyone desires to come after me, let him deny himself, and take (action and pick up) his cross daily and follow me." The next thing I want you to do, is look at the picture of the red and white striped cross made out of the roadblock. The red color stripes on the cross stand for the blood that He shed to remove your sin and bring salvation to you. While the white stripes on the cross symbolize your new life in the Lord, the forgiveness of sins. This is your hope that you can go forward improving your quality of life in every aspect. Once you've written down your positive plan of action on your "Go" worksheet, it means you are making a commitment before the Lord that you do not want to turn back to your old negative ways.

God's word says that once you ask forgiveness of your sins, He remembers them no more. He casts them into the sea, never to be remembered again. Isaiah 53:5 says, "By His stripes we are healed." That just doesn't mean physical healing, but spiritual healing as well. Forgiveness of sin, reunion with God! Great news isn't it! I want you to remember this too, the color red means, "Stop". So, whatever you are doing that is causing you not to have a relationship with your creator, your heavenly Father, *stop* doing it now! Give the Lord a chance! He was willing to take a chance on you. He gave His life for you. What greater friend than one who will give his own life for you?

List below three Positive ways, how you plan to take down your Roadblocks and go Forward.

1. _____
2. _____
3. _____

It is the battle within that we must win!

Let's take the story of the cross a little bit further. Most of us have heard the story of the wide path and narrow path pertaining to our spiritual walk with the Lord. The truth is that the Bible actually talks about a narrow gate and a wide gate in John 10. The wide gate is easier to get through, but the narrow gate is the way of life, the way of God. Suppose you were carrying the cross on your shoulders and the bottom part was dragging on the ground. What mark would that cross be leaving on the ground? It would be leaving a drag line, a narrow path behind the cross.

What is so interesting about that is the cross is a symbol to represent the action the Lord took to save all mankind. When you read John 10:1-9, He plainly states that He is the Keeper of the Gate. Therefore, it would be the narrow path of the cross' drag line that would lead us to the keeper of that narrow gate which leads us to His way of life that is good for us.

Once you've made a commitment to dedicate your heart and dreams to God, you will be able to move on with your life. It will renew your spiritual well-being as well as the physical realm of things in your life. Your self-will has to be greater than your weaknesses. Remember, the Word says, "Greater is He in me, than he that is in the world." I have learned that what my dad did cannot set the pace for me or control the quality of my life. I cannot blame myself for his actions, that he used to kill my mother and himself. I do not want his bad actions to control my life anymore, so everyday I have to live the Roadblock message I preach. One day, in 1999, I was lying in bed and feeling sorry for myself and all of a sudden, I saw a vision of a fighter jet fly over my bed fast and I said, to God, "What was that all about?" The Father said to me, "Quit feeling sorry for yourself! **It is the battle within that you must win!**" I realize then that I had to get up and get going and get the Roadblock message out fast! People needed to hear the message, so it could help them too, not just me. That is why I like the picture of the soldiers squatting down and coming up with a plan, together to fight the battle within us, because there is wisdom in seeking wise counseling. God never expected us to have to fight our battles alone. Sometimes our pride or shame prevents us from asking for help. The Lord did not carry His own cross to Calvary. A stranger from out of the crowd had to help him carry His burden. If your burdens are too heavy, it is time to tell someone and get help with them.

. . . By His strips we are healed

Isaiah 53:5

CHAPTER 17

Getting help

Getting help is just a phone call away. Asking a professional, a friend, family member and by praying to the Heavenly Father for wisdom, you too can come up with a survival plan. Sometimes pride, shame and other things can keep us bound in our circumstances or issues that we need to overcome, to keep a positive, healthy balance in our lives because we are worried what other people will think about us, if we admit that we need help. Asking for help is what the Lord did, because sometimes we all need help to carry our burdens. He set the perfect example of not being too prideful to let someone else carry your burden. So let go of the burden and let help come from other sources you may have not expected. Just like the Lord, my mother, and I did.

Not too long ago I was invited to speak at a woman's ministry that helps women that are coming out of abusive situations. One of the women in the class asked me if I had ever gotten professional help to overcome my dad's abuse. I explained to her that I have never gone to a professional counselor to overcome my family's' tragic past. I've always depended on the Heavenly Father to help me overcome all the baggage dumped on me by my dad's actions. I assure you if I ever felt I needed a professional counselor to talk to, I would have. I have had to work through it by reading books, going to hear other guest speakers, praying, going to church, speaking with friends and family that have overcome issues in their own lives. The greatest inspiration in my life today is the Heavenly Father and my mother. Though she is deceased, she is still a great inspiration for me to keep pushing forward and keep making positive choices for my life.

Chapter 18

What keeps me going?

What keeps me going? That is a very important question. What keeps me going, persevering and not letting my family's tragic past hold me back, is the hope, deep within my spirit that God has placed there. He has given me a peace, that surpasses all understanding. He has given me compassion in my heart, that has taught me to forgive those who have wronged me. To forgive someone, is a gift. It is giving compassion and grace where there was none. Can you think of a time in your life that you have done something you were not proud of and needed someone to have compassion to forgive you of your wrongs? The Word says, "Do unto others as you would have them do unto you."

Step-by-step, God has let me take down the roadblocks that have held me captive for far too long. I have learned to quit blaming others for my problems. I encourage others that have crossed my path, which are struggling with issues that are taking up to much of their time, to stop and take down the roadblocks and find peace with themselves, God and others. Hate can only bring destruction and relationship problems to your life, sometimes pushing those you love and care about away from you. Forgiveness means no longer letting that person or circumstance control your feelings and actions. Letting go of the negative things in our lives, means we have made a commitment to go forward in a positive manner, making good changes that effect not only us, but those around us too.

My hope is for you who are reading this book, that you will find hope and encouragement through my story. I sincerely pray that you will find the same peace I have in my life. I am nobody special. Just a faith believing woman who has shared her broken life from the past, with others, in hopes that anyone struggling with similar issues, that my story will help you put the negative past behind and move on with your life. Life is too short to live it sad and broken. May my story help you find closure to negative issues that have held you back and has kept you from meeting your destiny.

⁴ Then the word of the LORD came to me, saying:
⁵ "Before I formed you in the womb I knew you;
Before you were born I sanctified you;
I ordained you a prophet to the nations."

⁶ Then said I:
"Ah, Lord GOD!
Behold, I cannot speak, for I *am* a youth."

⁷ But the LORD said to me:
"Do not say, 'I *am* a youth,'
For you shall go to all to whom I send you,
And whatever I command you, you shall speak.
⁸ Do not be afraid of their faces,
For I *am* with you to deliver you," says the LORD.

Jeremiah 1 (New King James Version)

CHAPTER 19

Destiny

I know that my destiny is to share my story and the "Roadblock Message" with the world. It brings me great joy to help others let go of their sad and broken past, so they too can find their destiny, making a difference in this big world we live in.

I love it when I work with adults and youth of all ages, that feel they have no direction for their life. They don't know whether they are coming or going and it feels as if all hope is gone and they will never be happy again. Then, they go through the Roadblock class, they receive encouragement that brings about a positive, long-term change that they can incorporate into their everyday routine.

If you would like to schedule me to come and speak at your next meeting, conference, youth rally, youth group, adult bible studies, church services, camps, prisons, schools, and other events, you can contact me through my web site at: www.rbministry.com

My story and the "Roadblock Message" are designed to meet the needs of all groups. Both stories can be given as a faith-based or secular messages. Either way can still give the same powerful message of forgiveness and positive change, affecting the listener to find solutions to their negative issues and seeking peace with their troubled past.

When I share with children 7 to 12 years of age, I soften the words used to share my story. I use worksheets, arts and crafts, along with music and other visual materials. People of all ages need to be inspired, set-free from their broken past and even children need to know they to, have a destiny.

CHAPTER 20

Testimonies

I started Roadblock Ministry in 1999, when the Heavenly Father gave me the "Roadblock Message", I spoke of earlier. One of the things I enjoy about my ministry is the testimonies that are shared with me about how my story has helped others to bring positive change to their lives.

Not too long after I began Roadblock Ministry, I was invited to speak to a youth group on a Wednesday evening, in a church near Fort Worth, Texas. After the class, a teenage boy came forward and asked for prayer and help to quit doing drugs. I am so glad that he saw how God wanted to him to change his life for the positive.

I was invited to speak to a youth group in a local church. A couple weeks after I had been there, I received a phone call from a woman telling me about a teenage girl that heard me speak that night. She said," the youth pastor was not even on the subject of roadblocks and the teenage girl stood up and asked if she could share her story after hearing the guest speaker, Val Henderson." The youth pastor said, "yes", she could share her story. The girl told how she came to forgive her dad and mother for divorcing each other and how she was able to forgive her stepmother for marrying her dad. She invited her dad, stepmother and younger brother to church that following Sunday. Then when the girl was through sharing her story of forgiveness, a teenage boy stood up and said, "While we are the subject, I'd like to share what happened to me after the roadblock message. I was able to forgive myself for something I did. I had been struggling with forgiving myself for a long time and now I've learned to forgive myself." Wow! God is awesome! He knows what we need and when we need it.

Another interesting story I like to share was a phone call I had received from a young woman in her mid twenty's. She heard me speak at a youth group in Fort Worth, Texas.

She told me when she got home that Sunday afternoon, that she went to her bedroom and kneeled down before the Heavenly Father and started praying to Him to find out what her roadblocks were. What He told her was that "the tongue ring she had in her mouth was a roadblock and it was keeping her moving forward in the business world." The young woman said, she took out the tongue ring that day and never has put it back in.

In another church I was invite to. I spoke to the youth group on a Sunday morning and the adults on a Wednesday night. It was powerful what happened afterwards, with both the adults and youth. There was this little boy about 8 or 9 years old. He came into the class with his arms inside his shirt. His mother had tried to convince him to take his arms out of his shirt before he came into the Sunday school classroom.

His mother apologized to me. I said to her, looking at her son, "Don't worry, he will take his arms out of his shirt when we start having fun doing the arts and crafts, he is going to be able to make a roadblock and color the strips on it." The boy just looked at me and smiled as if to tell me, he'd think about taking his arms out of his shirt when we got to the arts and crafts. Well, needless to say, the boy took his arms out of his shirt when it came to arts and craft time.

On Wednesday evening, I was standing at the back of the church talking to the pastor and his wife. The little boy's mother came rushing up to me and said," Do you remember my son, he was the one that would not take his arms out of shirt, I am his mother." I said, "Yes." The woman continued on, "He came home on Sunday after church and explained to me your story and the roadblock message." Afterwards, he told me he had learned to forgive his dad, because his dad was in prison and not at home help raising him. He wanted his dad to be home and be in his life." I told her that was," Wonderful news to hear!"

After I finished speaking that night, a man came up to me and told me that he thought the reason God wanted him to hear my story, was that he probably needed to forgive his mothers murderer too. He was four years old at the time and living in another state. I said to him, "Isn't that amazing, God brought you all the way from another state, to live in Texas, so that you could hear my story. And that you could see your need to forgive your mother's murderer. There is a season and reason for everything that happens in our lives. I do not believe in coincidence or just by chance.

A pastor and his wife invited me to their Saturday morning service to be their guest speaker. It was pretty incredible because they were separated. They were having marital relationship problems. When I finished the service, I sat down with the pastor, his wife and the entire adult members that attended that gathering, to visit with them about the message I had just delivered on roadblocks and forgiveness. What happened next was so unexpected. The members opened up and shared with the pastor and his wife how they felt about them being separated and how their marriage problems were effecting the group. That morning we had accomplished quite a bit. It helped the church members to be able to express their feelings about the situation and that they were all wanting them to resolve their issues and get back together.

The next day, on Sunday, I received a phone call from the pastor's wife. She said, "Val late last night, my husband and I got back together. We spent hours on the phone talking about our roadblocks and finally, it was around midnight and we were still on the phone talking and I said to him, "Honey, come back home, I miss you and love you." Once again, God used a simple message to help two broken hearts to see the need to forgive, move forward and leave the roadblocks of the past behind.

Notes

Notes

United States Postal Service®
DELIVERY CONFIRMATION™

0312 1430 0001 4190 6007

UNITED STATES
POSTAL SERVICE

1000

48433

U.S. POSTAGE
PAID
KELLER.TX
76248
SEP 05. 12
AMOUNT

$3.48

00083106-01

CPSIA information can be obtained at www.ICGtesting.com
Printed in the USA
LVOW081457280112

265930LV00001B/51/P

9 781450 077156